Truth
By Nina Yau

First published in 2012
Copyright © 2012 by Nina Yau
Cover design and photography by flynnworks (www.flynnworks.com)
Layout design and typesetting by Airstrike Quintet (www.airstrikequintet.com)

ISBN: 978-0-9855770-0-1

dedicated to all seekers of the Truth

"It takes two to speak the truth—one to speak and another to hear."

—Henry David Thoreau

AUTHOR'S NOTE

It was October 2010, a rainy, gloomy weekday morning during the thick expanse of rush hour traffic in Chicago. I had taken the El train for thirty-five minutes, then a PACE bus for another twenty-five that dropped me off at the closest street corner it would come near the headquarters of the company I worked for, and I walked the next fifteen minutes.

In mid-gait, I stopped walking and looked up at the cloud-filled, gray sky, its looming darkness threatening the onslaught of a very wet and powerful storm. A large raindrop landed on my eyelid as I blinked it off, realizing an umbrella would have been wise to bring. Shrugging it off, I returned my gaze forward and continued walking towards the office.

It was during these fifteen minutes walking in the rain that I repeated to myself the Truth I had recently embraced as part of my life philosophy: no matter what it takes, I *will* live my life fearlessly, being audacious enough to take risks, for, at the very end of my life, I want to have died knowing I was truthful to others and, most especially, to the person in the mirror.

As I was repeating this mantra to myself, I was heading into a place my heart never loved. I had to chuckle at this irony, but I was prepared. I had written my resignation letter. I had made a promise to myself that I would stick by what I believed to be important in my life. I had a vision. And I was ready to go down in flames to carry out this vision if need be.

Truth is, I didn't go down in flames. I *am* the flame. I was always the fire. Truth just helped spark it into who I am today: totally and completely me.

On the third day of August 2011, I had *veritas*, the Latin word for Truth, tattooed onto my right shoulder blade. With the personal commitment I've made to Truth, I know that Truth will only meet me when I am ready to meet Truth.

Nina Yau

January 2012
Bangalore, India

The absence of Truth is death to your Soul.

Truth is not concerned with what's wrong or right. Labels do not matter.

Assigning a value to Truth is superfluous, for Truth cannot be assigned. It must be explored. It must be discovered and uncovered. It must be felt, not merely understood intellectually, but felt with your entire heart, your entire being. There is nothing deeper in matters of the heart than Truth itself.

Let's go exploring. Open mind, open heart. Truth awaits us all.

CHAPTER ONE
Philosophia

Philosophy is Truth. The word philosophy is derived from the Greek word *philosophia*, which means "love of wisdom."

There are many branches of philosophy, perhaps as many as there are languages in the world. Each thing, activity, way of life, viewpoint, belief, attitude and value system can be construed as philosophy. It simply depends on the individual.

There are various academic branches of philosophy but, when one thinks of it, life itself is one continuous philosophy. We are searching.

Until we know what we are searching for and, thus, pursue it without hesitation, we are in limbo. We are stagnant, in a state of flux. We remain suspended in time, in a perpetual state of inertia without actually going anywhere.

Level and ground yourself. Go inward. Search deeper, search with purpose, search with inner wisdom. The Truth is within us all.

CHAPTER TWO
What is your Truth level?

Robert M. Pirsig wrote in *Zen and the Art of Motorcycle Maintenance*, "We have many different answers to the same question, all of which can be thought of as true within their own context."

We all have our own Truth level. Your Truth level is the point in which you consciously, subconsciously and unconsciously decide to open yourself up. To the universe, to others and to yourself.

Your Truth level is whatever natural state you are currently in. Everyone's Truth level is distinctive, for everyone experiences life differently.

We all must be aware of our current Truth level. The moment we dip too low, we start to feel indifferent about ourselves. We may not even recognize who the person in the mirror is. This is when you no longer do things for your heart's desire but, rather, you do things out of complacency, normalcy or apathetic acceptance. This is a dangerous place to be, for you are no longer listening to yourself.

You cannot overdose on Truth. You cannot exceed the maximum, for there is no maximum. There is only the void you feel the moment you aren't being honest with yourself.

What is your Truth level?

CHAPTER THREE
Running Away / Towards Yourself

So true funny how it seems
Always in time, but never in line for dreams.
Head over heels when toe-to-toe.
This is the sound of my soul,
This is the sound
I bought a ticket to the world
But now I've come back again
Why do I find it hard to write the next line?
Oh I want the truth to be said

—Spandau Ballet, *True*

You need not flee from the very person who can love you the most in this entire world: yourself.

Naturally, this means you are the very person who can hate yourself the most. There is no white without black. There is no sun without the moon. There is no summer without winter. There is no ice without water. There is no shatter without the glass.

There must be a definitive balance between this love/hate relationship we all have within us.

Are we running away or running towards ourselves?

What are the actions we are doing or not doing that are causing us to drift further away or towards our true selves? What do you need to address today?

Some people believe that traveling nomads, independent wanderers of our lovely generation, modern-day vagabonds and hobos, are running away from themselves. And for some of these travelers, they are.

I've met a number of travelers and backpackers who are simply opting to run away from their problems, run away from uncomfortable situations, run away from facing themselves, by immersing their bodies and minds in the rush of traveling from one place to another, one country to another. They feel safe and comfortable in the active motions of going from point A to point B, but what they have neglected is to find point C. That point is themselves. That point is the Truth.

While out on a small bamboo fishing boat in Inle Lake, Myanmar (formerly Burma), I met a middle-aged American woman who expressed to me how sad it was that not many Americans travel to far-reaching countries.

She remarked that because of traveling, she was able to find more of herself. To self-explore, to self-discover. To realize more of her inner world and how that was juxtaposed with the world around her.

I couldn't agree more.

People do things for deeper reasons than what may be obvious. We don't just travel for travel's sake, to stamp our passports with another foreign inkblot, in various colors, characters and languages. We travel because we cannot help but let the world show us for who we really are.

Like Ray Bradbury said in *Fahrenheit 451*, "Stuff your eyes with wonder; live as if you'd drop dead in ten seconds. See the world. It's more fantastic than any dream made or paid for in factories."

Don't run away just because things get rough. Don't numb yourself because you are uncomfortable. Stop running, face yourself and seek the Truth within. You may discover you are stronger than you think.

CHAPTER FOUR
Self-Honesty and Being in the Present

Ayn Rand writes in *Atlas Shrugged*, "Let go—drop the controls—this is it."

Being honest with yourself is one of the deepest Truths you can explore. It is a shame more people aren't honest with themselves. It is an even deeper shame when they don't even know who they really are, what they are put on this Earth to do (or even more simply, to be), why they are even here, living, breathing, shaking, dying.

A Sufi quote says, "You want to know why you are here? You are here to find out what is real."

Remember who you are and what you came here to do.

Ask yourself these two questions right now:

1. Why am I here?
2. What am I doing with my life?

Be honest with yourself. There is no one to judge or condemn you. These are some of the most private and intimate questions you shall ever ask of yourself. No answers, including non-answers, are wrong. Why assign a "wrong" or "right"? Your answers simply are your Truth.

Life is a constant experiment. There is no failure; there is only experimentation. You need not fear not succeeding in life, because life simply is.

Sitting becomes just sitting. Breathing becomes just breathing.

There is beauty and poetry in this.

Life is today. It is not yesterday. It is not even tomorrow. The present is all we have.

CHAPTER FIVE
Evolution ⟷ Progression

Without evolution, we cannot progress. Without progression, we cannot evolve.

To not grow is to die. Man will always die physical deaths; this is without question. Mental, emotional and spiritual deaths may come much sooner than our physical deaths, however, due to improper attention towards things that do not matter.

Rather than cutting wide, let us cut deep.
Rather than breadth, let us go for depth.
Rather than many, let's have few.

Superficiality and commercial value are not progression. Fleeting trends, fashion and glamour, fame, vanity, external appearances, social proof, obsession with money, power and ego, all lead towards self-destruction. Though these things may initially create feelings of self-appreciation and self-worth, they do not come without a price on one's soul.

Strip away the arbitrary complexities and feel your present being. Where are you at today?

Are you happy?
Are you healthy?
Are you loved?
Do you love?

Truth is love. Love is Truth.

You are love. You are Truth.

CHAPTER SIX
Evolve By Reduction

There are only a few things you really need once you decide to move on. What you'll require wherever you land. Fine suit of clothing. The tools of your trade. And some token of your past, a reminder of who you really are. Everything else, you just don't need.

—Dexter Morgan, *Dexter*

The truth of the matter is, we do not need much to get by in life.

Some say you need money. Yes—to a certain extent.
Some say you need a career. Yes—to a certain extent.
Some say you need a life partner. Yes—to a certain extent.
Some say you need a home/vehicle/phone/Internet. Yes—to a certain extent.

Eliminate the extraneous and what do you have left? The essentials. The extraordinary. Simply you. This is what matters.

You can evolve yourself by continually reducing life to its basic necessities. For most, this is shelter, clothing and food. The intangibles would consist of love, trust, respect, light, growth, adventure, discovery, awareness and meaning.

Rid yourself of all that is unnecessary. Modern society has proclaimed we need the latest and greatest technological gadgets man has created thus far, leading us to look a specific part in order to fulfill a defined role. The question is, if we have survived and done perfectly well in the past without these revolutionary inventions and external validations, why are we suddenly ill content with what we do not have?

We must be mindful of our consumption habits. Without mindfulness, we are only drifting, from one fad, habit, thought, location or person to another. Don't drift mindlessly. Travel with purpose instead.

Look around you. There is water; there is greenery; there is life in the air, on the ground and in the oceans. There is so much in this world. Everything we would ever need or want, we already have.

Look at yourself and realize your abundance. You have your body. You have your mind. You have the ability to read these words, right at this very minute. You have love in at least one of its many forms. Even if all you have in the entire world is your dog or cat that's lying down next to you, you already experience immense love in this world. You are love.

CHAPTER SEVEN
Empty Your Head. I Am Ready to Pour.

Man believes he knows many things. When we share mindlessly a litany of facts, figures and statistics, showcasing our supreme knowledge, academic prowess or the ability to intellectually philosophize, we are inadvertently feeding our ego and pride.

I am reminded of a beautiful Zen tale, which I would like to share with you here:

Once upon a time, there lived a Zen master named Nansen.

There also lived a professor of philosophy. One day, the professor was walking wearily in his travels and came across Nansen's cottage.

Nansen invited the professor into his home and said, "Wait a little."

The professor looked to be in a hurry, but Nansen said, "I will prepare tea for you. You look tired. Wait a little, rest a little and have a cup of tea. Then we can discuss."

Nansen started boiling the water and at the same time looked over to the professor. While the water was boiling, he saw the professor was boiling within too.

Not only was the teakettle making sounds as the water boiled, the professor was making more sounds within, chattering and continuously talking. The professor was preparing himself—what to ask, how to ask and from where to begin.

Nansen smiled to himself while watching the professor and thought, "This man is too full, so much so that nothing can enter him. The answer cannot be given because there is no one to receive it. The guest cannot enter into the house—there is no room."

Out of compassion, Nansen wanted to become a guest in this professor. He knocks from everywhere but there is no door. And even if he breaks down a door, there is no room. The professor was so full; he could not even enter within himself. He sits outside of his own being, just on the steps, unable to enter.

Nansen poured the tea into the cup. The professor became uneasy as Nansen continuously poured the tea into the cup. It was overflowing; soon, it would be spilling onto the floor.

The professor then said, "Stop! What are you doing? This cup cannot hold any more tea, not even a single drop. Are you mad? What are you doing?"

Nansen smiled at the professor and replied, "The same is the case with you. You are so alert to observe and become aware that the cup is full and cannot hold any more, why are you not so aware about your own self? You are overflowing with opinions, philosophies, doctrines and scriptures. You know too much already; I cannot give you anything. You have traveled in vain. Before coming to me you should have emptied your cup, then I could pour something into it."

What Nansen was saying to the professor was, "Empty your head. I am ready to pour."

Do not assume you know everything. Do not assume you know anything.

Only when you empty your head can the world and your higher self begin to teach you.

CHAPTER EIGHT
The Art of Zazen

At the heart of Japanese Zen Buddhist practice, martial artists, warriors, samurais and Zen practitioners understand the fundamental need and spiritual thirst for *zazen*. *Zazen*, a Japanese word, aims to open the hand of thought and is the simple seated meditation discipline which all students of the way practice.

As a martial artist, I sit in *zazen* before and after training. As a yogi, I sit in *sukhasana* (easy pose, or cross-legged pose) or *ardha padmasana* (half lotus pose).

It is not only essential for the body to relax before the start of learning something new or practicing an ancient form, but it is imperative for the mind to empty itself. By suspending all thinking, entering the state of nonthinking, we leave all transgressions at the door, all worries by the wayside, all meandering thoughts, and all stress and anxieties where we first picked them up.

Without *zazen*, one is never fully present.

Zazen is practiced in one of three ways:

1. Concentration

Focus on your breath, breathing from the *hara* (the center of gravity in your belly). Ideally, you want to experience *dhyana*, or one-pointedness of mind. Concentrate.

2. *Koan* Introspection

A *koan* is a story, dialogue, question or statement in which the meaning cannot be understood by rational thinking but, rather, intuition.

An example of a *koan*:

A monk asked Zhaozhou, "Does a dog have Buddha nature or not?" Zhaozhou said, "*Wú.*"

(*Wú* in Chinese means "not," "nothing," "non being," or simply as "no thing.")

In *koan* introspection, one must transcend reality beyond thinking of the rational. This may not come easy for the practical or logical person but with developed practice and focused concentration, it is very possible.

3. *Shikantaza* (just sitting)

Dogen Zenji, a Japanese Zen Buddhist teacher (1200-1253) and founder of the Soto order, wrote in *Shobogenzo* (*Treasury of the True Dharma Eye*), "Sitting fixedly, think of not thinking. How do you think of not thinking? Nonthinking. This is the art of *zazen*."

You simply sit, with no objective or goal, allowing yourself to remain fully aware and present in the moment. Focus on your inhalation and exhalation. There is nothing, just now.

It would be absolutely transformative if we all took up this ancient practice of meditation. No matter who you are, where you come from, what you did in the past and present, what your future holds in store for you, meditation is for everyone.

For your mind. For your body. For your heart. For your spirit.

CHAPTER NINE
The Violence That Busyness Perpetuates

Time weighs down on you like an old, ambiguous dream. You keep on moving, trying to slip through it. But even if you go to the ends of the earth, you won't be able to. Still, you have to go there—to the edge of the world. There's something you can't do unless you get there.

—Haruki Murakami, *Kafka on the Shore*

Our everyday lives are increasingly busier. We are forever obsessed with production, efficiency, just-in-time management techniques, multi-tasking and churning out as much as possible in as little time as possible.

We are in the age of the efficiency epidemic.

Being busy, at surface level, may feel empowering and worthwhile. You feel like you are being productive, you feel like you are important, you feel like you are not wasting time, you feel like you are not being lazy.

Jack Kerouac wrote in *The Dharma Bums*, "[Alvah] was always being bugged by my little lectures on Samadhi ecstasy, which is the state you reach when you stop everything and stop your mind and you actually with your eyes closed see a kind of eternal multiswarm of electrical Power of some kind ululating in place of just pitiful images and forms of objects, which are, after all, imaginary. And if you don't believe me come back in a billion years and deny it. For what is time?"

What is time?

Time simply is. There is no waste. There is no more to be added. Time is a cup filled to the top with tea. Nothing can be added. You can only take away.

Yes, what you do with your time is essential, for some activities weigh heavier in your life and soul's purpose than others.

But jam-packing your day-to-day life is futile. It is, in fact, violence upon your soul. Thrashing your fragile body around and around, until it's run down to the ground, completely exhausted and trampled upon. This is not productivity; this is a slow and painful pre-mature death.

Let us stop the needless violence. Let us love ourselves. Let us quiet our hearts, listen to the self, and find the Truth that resides in us all.

We need not be busy in order to feel important. You already are important. If you're in this world right now, you are important.

CHAPTER TEN
Our Own Flaws

What man loathes in other people is oftentimes what he loathes in himself. That which causes him to recoil in anger, frustration, contempt and hatred can be the very thing he must address within himself.

An unforgiving focus and attention to detail may give man great accuracy in life but it may also cause him to lose sight of the bigger picture. Stroking one's ego ought not drive all our actions in life. The honest man will not destroy others in order to build himself up. Success in life is not dependent upon comparison and competition with others.

A weak man becomes riled up and detests all others who show him what his true face really is, and that is the lack of binding strength that the strong man has and the weak one does not. We are all reflections of one another. When someone reflects back to you your own flaws, the strong man accepts this truth and does not recoil from it, whereas the weak man asserts blame upon others. Essentially, he is running away from the truth.

When one shouts obscenities at you, this reveals his true character rather than yours. Remember to stand up and disengage yourself from this baited attack. This will disarm the attacker. His character is in question here, not yours. Those who judge you and their judgments are to be of no concern to you.

Let us self-examine intently and with sincerity. Hiding from ourselves is defeating, for who will judge you? No one but you alone.

CHAPTER ELEVEN
The Highest Responsibility You Shall Ever Have

The highest responsibility you shall ever have in this world is for your own life. It is higher than your career, than being a mother or father, than your education, than your civil duties, than anything else.

We may be born from our mother's womb and feel eternal biological obligation to our blood family as a result, but do not forget that our family members shall regard their own selves as the ultimate priority, whether they speak this truth or not.

When man gets a bloody gash on his leg, is it not a human instinct that he will want to clean the wound and bandage it properly? Typically, this instinct will come before addressing someone else's wounds. Lest the person has altruism weaved into the very fabric of his being, man will naturally have self-attending tendencies.

Is this wrong or is this right? Why even assign a "wrong" or a "right" to this matter? Let it just be, much like a stream flows with water.

Do we ask the stream if it is wrong or right to flow with water? Of course not. It just is.

CHAPTER TWELVE
Give Me Truth

'Men,' said the little prince, 'crowd into express trains without knowing what they are looking for. So they become agitated and rush round in circles...' After a pause, he added: 'It is not worth the trouble.'

—Antoine De Saint-Exupery, *The Little Prince*

Man, in the end, wants the same things.

To some degree, we all want Truth, Meaning, Freedom, Love, Happiness, Adventure, Peace. There are many more things, of course, but in the end, we all want the same things. We just go about getting them in different ways.

To attain Freedom and Peace, man will wage wars, killing one another without mercy or remorse.

To attain Financial Success, man will cheat, accept bribes or cut corners, justifying it by saying, "If I don't do this, the next guy will and he'll have gotten something for it." It's as if being Good does not matter as much as being Better does.

"So long as I'm better off than Joe Blow, I'm happy," is a thought that crosses his mind. But remove comparison, remove approval sought from others, remove superficial goals and perceived success in society's eyes, remove expectations, and what do you have? You have Truth.

Henry David Thoreau wrote in *Walden*, "Rather than love, than money, than fame, give me truth. I sat at a table where were rich food and wine in abundance, but sincerity and truth were not; and I went away hungry, from the inhospitable board. The hospitality was as cold as the ices."

Measuring our self-worth based on external validations, social proof, success standards, material and financial wealth, vanity, the pedigree of our academic training and the like, is a self-defeating cycle which we will always remain trapped in lest we truly open our eyes to the eternal Truth that is within us.

CHAPTER THIRTEEN
No Permanence, Only Fluidity

According to Sufi master Abdul Kadar, the body is a microcosm of the natural world. The natural elements have their homologous elements in our experience—sneezing is like an earthquake, a shout like thunder, crying like rain and tears like salt water: 'First one must understand the body as part of the earth and the natural laws thereof. All the powers of the outside world are manifest in you.'

—Phillip B. Zarrilli, *When the Body Becomes All Eyes*

Our lives are ever changing, ever flowing. There is no permanence, only fluidity.

Those who have accepted their lives as one that cannot be changed, whether their reasons are because of circumstances, upbringing, social status, economic standing, geographical and cultural influences, do not realize, or have chosen to ignore, that the course of one's life is, to many extents, a result of the choices one makes.

Our obligation and purpose in life ought to be our driving mission, a sole mission that no one else is responsible for.

CHAPTER FOURTEEN
Trust In Truth

Boy: "Do not try and bend the spoon. That's impossible. Instead, only try to realize the truth."
Neo: "What truth?"
Boy: "There is no spoon."
Neo: "There is no spoon?"
Boy: "Then you'll see that it is not the spoon that bends. It is only yourself."

—The Matrix

Trust is an action as well as a belief.

Do you believe in your actions?
Do you believe in the strength of human abilities?
Do you believe in the firm grasp you have on Truth and, as a result, the firm grasp Truth has on you?

What do you trust in? What do you believe in?

Is it…

—your country?
—your religion?
—your practice?
—your philosophy?
—your mind?

—your body?
—your dwelling?
—your language?
—your style?
—your love?
—your intuition?
—your work?
—your art?
—your partner?
—your family?
—your neighbor?
—your world?
—your self?

What do you trust in? What do you believe in?

Some people avoid their inherent Truths, such as natural talents and gifts, their ethnic origin, and so forth. Some may believe their talents are actually a curse. They aren't.

Embrace who you really are. Embrace your Truth.

CHAPTER FIFTEEN
Truth's Opposite

Surface, surface, surface was all that anyone found meaning in...this was civilization as I saw it, colossal and jagged...

—Patrick Bateman, Bret Easton Ellis' *American Psycho*

The opposite of Truth is falseness, falsity, untruth, nontruth or ignorance.

Untruth is different than lies. When lies are spoken, a person has made a choice not to speak the Truth and, instead, speak of something else entirely, while still knowing what the Truth is.

When Truth is concealed and quickly replaced with superficiality, external motivating factors, or quick-gain, short-term results, there is something terribly amiss.

Truth becomes the black that should have been the white.
It becomes the low that should have been the high.
It becomes the stagnant that should have been the flowing.
It becomes the dark that should have been the light.

But without the opposite of Truth, how do we savor and appreciate it when Truth looks us in the eye, asking us with genuine love and sincerity, "Why do you look elsewhere? I am Here."

CHAPTER SIXTEEN
Minimalism Transcended

People had more than they needed. We had no idea what was precious, what wasn't. We threw away things people kill each other for now.

—Eli, *The Book of Eli*

Minimalism, at first glance, is oftentimes considered an aesthetic appeal to the natural state of being, as in, a minimalist approach in design, visual art, architecture, fashion and music.

This is true, certainly.

But minimalism can go much deeper, if one seeks that depth consciously.

Minimalism can evolve you but only if you choose to evolve minimalism as it fits your life. Asking yourself, "What is essential?" is a wonderful question that probes deeper into your specific life's core Truth.

You can transcend minimalism into a way of life, a philosophy, a conscious and meditative practice.

All your actions become vital, for you no longer allow the nonessentials into your daily activities. All your choices become imperative, for you no longer allow the non-sensical into your daily decision-making. All your viewpoints and stances become core-driven, for you no longer allow the superficial to exist in your life's daily walk.

Minimalism, then, is no longer simply an aesthetic choice or a popular, environmentally friendly movement.

It becomes the way, the only way.

Truth seeks the heart of what matters. It does not look drastically different than minimalism, for both drive deep.

CHAPTER SEVENTEEN
Essence Extracted

You are this.

—Buddha

Truth is sincerity in action and character. The essence of language, culture, people, land, innovation, invention, government, philosophy, et cetera, is extracted.

Nothing is added and nothing is taken away.

Truth is a state of being. Frivolous states of affairs are eschewed for Truth.

This is what matters.

CHAPTER EIGHTEEN
5-7-5

Effortlessly observing the self's movements in accordance to the environment and the environment's movements in accordance with the self, one can begin to have a broader understanding of Nature as she has intended. We live side-by-side with a billion living things all around us. Yet sometimes, we become so engrossed in our own mind's activities that we forget that all around us, poetry and the song of Nature are freely there, gently reminding us that every single thing exists for the sheer pleasure of it. It needn't have to make sense, to have things go a certain way, our way, really.

We simply need to open our eyes, heart outstretched, and observe.

—Nina Yau, *Human Nature*

illuminating
essences of Truth that are
forever with us.

"follow me," It says,
rivers flowing, take me with
on its back, on you.

wildfire, burning
flames flicker in the distance;
tend to it, the Truth.

30 | TRUTH

house of braves cry out,
by the rope ye shall be hanged,
"exit, this untruth!"

embody the Truth
let it take control of you
release, and be free.

Truth in Truth in Truth
upside our heads, spinning round,
"here I am!" It cries.

lies, you once believed;
sit me down, we need to talk,
question, "who are we?"

CHAPTER NINETEEN
Shoshin

In Zen Buddhism and the Japanese martial arts, *shoshin* means beginner's mind, as well as "correct Truth."

Shoshin is an attitude of openness. It is an attitude of eagerness, to approach each new venture, day, subject or person, with humility and a gracious, humble outlook.

There is no room for the person who thinks she knows all.

In *Zen Mind, Beginner's Mind,* Zen master Shunryu Suzuki wrote, "In the beginner's mind there are many possibilities, in the expert's mind there are few."

In order to seek Truth, in order to receive Truth, one must not approach Truth-seeking, Truth-receiving, with a position of close-mindedness and expectancy. Essentially, one mustn't allow oneself to keep an expert mind.

Like the Zen tale of master Nansen, empty your mind. Truth is ready to pour.

CHAPTER TWENTY
Satya

Satya is Sanskrit that means Truth. In philosophy, the meaning of the word *satya* is unchangeable, or that which pervades the universe in all its constancy, or that which has no distortion.

Satya pertains to everything and anything concerning the ultimate Truth and Truth in all its glorious components.

An ancient Sanskrit proverb goes something like this: Truth triumphs eventually.

Read that again, slowly this time:

Truth.
Triumphs.
Eventually.

Breaking this down, we first have Truth.

Truth; noun; the quality or state of being true; that which is true or in accordance with fact or reality.

Let's move on to the next word: triumphs.

Triumph; noun and verb; a great victory or achievement; to achieve a victory or be successful.

Truth triumphs, but of what?

Truth can triumph...

—Hate
—Despair
—Ignorance
—Shallowness
—Mindlessness
—Greed
—Fear
—Knowledge
—Destruction
—Creation
—Self

And finally, the third word: eventually.

Eventually; adverb; in the end, especially after a long delay, dispute or series of problems.

Truth triumphs *eventually*.

This means, until Truth triumphs, we are faced with myriad obstacles and challenges, problems, situations, ideas, visions, promises and people, which can all potentially lead us down a false path.

Until Truth triumphs eventually, let us remain strong, ever present, honest and Truth-focused.

To drive to the core of what matters, one needs to practice patience. Patience is not something one is born with or one can inherit. Patience is the capacity to accept or tolerate delay, trouble or suffering *without* the act of becoming upset.

So until Truth triumphs eventually, remain patient, all the while deflecting false idols, paths, assurances and acceptances for what is initially seen and considered to be the Truth.

Our beliefs can waver, our common sense not so common, our senses faltering, our tempers tested, our difficulties heightened.

Remain steadfast in your Truth-seeking journey. Truth will, eventually, triumph all.

CHAPTER TWENTY-ONE
Satyagraha

Satyagraha, Sanskrit for an insistence on Truth, was conceived and developed by Mahatma Gandhi during the Indian independence movement and his earlier struggles in South Africa.

Gandhi said, "I have also called it love-force or soul-force. In the application of *satyagraha*, I discovered in the earliest stages that pursuit of truth did not admit of violence being inflicted on one's opponent but that he must be weaned from error by patience and compassion. For what appears to be truth to the one may appear to be error to the other. And patience means self-suffering. So the doctrine came to mean vindication of truth, not by infliction of suffering on the opponent, but on oneself."

Those who practice *satyagraha* or, simply, those who practice the love-force, are called *satyagrahis*.

Truth is love. This love-force Gandhi refers to is within us all. But it is up to us to choose this practice as a way of life.

CHAPTER TWENTY-TWO
真相

Truth, in traditional Mandarin Chinese, is 真相, pronounced *zhenxiang*.

Reflect upon this ancient Chinese proverb:

星星之火可以燎原 (*xingxing zhi huo keyi liaoyuan*)
A spark can start a fire that burns the entire prairie.

Morally, this means do not underestimate the potential destructive power that a seemingly minor problem can cause. A butterfly beats its wings in America and starts a hurricane in China.

One small act can produce another act which produces another act which produces yet another act.

Truth, if not consciously and deliberately pursued with raw and honest intention, can lead to subtle, negative (or stagnant) acts that produce more of the same kind. Subtlety is unnoticeable, at first. That's why it's subtle. But over time, these thoughts become habitual and, eventually, become your life.

CHAPTER TWENTY-THREE
Truth In Work

When Aristotle said, "We are what we do repeatedly," this beckons the question, What are we doing? And beyond that, *How* are we going about doing that thing that we do?

Is it with trust? Honesty? Mindfulness? Quality? Purpose?

When you do your work, create your art, do it with purpose, create with intention.

There is no point in seeking short-term gains by means of cutting corners for, in the end, it is our actions that dictate who we are and what we fundamentally believe to be important in our lives.

Work truthfully. There is no better time than now to be honest with yourself in your work.

CHAPTER TWENTY-FOUR
On Bullshit

Harry G. Frankfurt, renowned moral philosopher at Princeton University, wrote a thought-provoking essay called *On Bullshit*.

What does bullshit mean? What does it entail? Who would employ the use of bullshit and why? Is bullshit an opponent of Truth? Or is it a by-product of the Truth's opposite core? Is it necessary, at times, to "bullshit" others, including the self?

Frankfurt wrote, "Is the bullshitter by his very nature a mindless slob? Is his product necessarily messy or unrefined? The word shit does, to be sure, suggest this. Excrement is not designed or crafted at all; it is merely emitted, or dumped. It may have a more or less coherent shape, or it may not, but it is in any case certainly not *wrought*."

Bullshit is like hot air. It contains no sustenance and nothing substantial. There is nothing within it of use.

Bullshit is a barrier to Truth. It is not the same as lies. Lying suggests that the person knows the Truth but chooses not to speak it and, rather, speaks of something else that is not the Truth.

In your work, art, practice, relationships, inner dialogue and life direction, are you bullshitting yourself and those around you?

CHAPTER TWENTY-FIVE
Are you a Truth-seeker?

Two years he walks the earth. No phone, no pool, no pets, no cigarettes. Ultimate freedom. An extremist. An aesthetic voyager whose home is the road. Escaped from Atlanta. Thou shalt not return, 'cause "The West is the Best." And now after two rambling years comes the final and greatest adventure. The climactic battle to kill the false being within and victoriously conclude the spiritual revolution. Ten days and nights of freight trains and hitchhiking bring him to the great white North. No longer to be poisoned by civilization he flees, and walks alone upon the land to become <u>lost in the wild</u>.

—Alexander Supertramp (Christopher Johnson McCandless), May 1992, inscribed onto a piece of weathered plywood found on the Magic Bus

A Truth-seeker is a committed individual whose thirst for purity in wisdom, the heart of what matters and the essence of a purposeful life drives such individual to continually search for Truth in all she does, thinks and is.

She is a designer of her world by allowing the world to design her with Truth. Nothing is forsaken, for there is no better way in life than the pure path of Truth.

Are you a Truth-seeker?

You may be one if you:

—constantly search for meaning behind the action
—ask yourself why before you do something
—deliberately meet with yourself

—are mindful, in thought and action
—self-reflect and go within, allowing your heart's inner wisdom to guide you
—no longer care for label or role assignment, but rather, what is honest
—evaluate your place in life and how you are defining your world
—do not agree without consideration of what is best, not what is new or popular
—are honest with other human beings
—are honest with yourself

If you do not embody these characteristics (yet), do not fear.

Life is not a race; there is no final destination. There are no winners and losers, and this isn't a game where one side must be defeated by another. No battles exist except for the ones we create within ourselves. These are invisible fights, struggles for a more truthful life against a false one. The moment you give this up, this internal and eternal battle, is the moment you start walking the path of Truth. You then become a Truth-seeker.

Swami Veda Bharati, formerly known as Pandit Usharbudh Arya, wrote in *Philsophy of Hatha Yoga*, "A truth-seeker is one in whom mind, speech, and body all act together, in unison. In fact, in the ancient tradition, one of the definitions of personal truth, in terms of truthful speech and truthful acts, is that 'What one thinks with the mind, that one utters with the speech; what one utters with the speech, that one puts into action; what one thus puts into action is accomplished and fulfilled.' The entire personality is involved."

Truth is embodied when one seeks it and applies it to one's life wholeheartedly. Seek the Truth with earnestness, sincerity and authenticity. You have it within you; it has always been there. Align the mind, body and spirit to seek the Truth together.

This is the way of the Truth-seeker.

CHAPTER TWENTY-SIX
Truth Questions

Robert M. Pirsig, author of *Zen and the Art of Motorcycle Maintenance*, asks terrific questions.

For instance, he wrote, "What is the truth and how do you know it when you have it?... How do we really know anything? Is there an 'I,' a 'soul,' which knows, or is this soul merely cells coordinating senses?...Is reality basically changing, or is it fixed and permanent?...When it's said that something means something, what's meant by that?"

Below are questions you must not be afraid to ask yourself—and answer honestly—when seeking Truth.

Sit with these. Meditate on them. Answers need not come right away. They may never come at all. Be alright with this. Allow yourself introspection and reflection.

What is Truth to me?

What am I doing to cultivate Truth in my life?

What are my absolute essential needs in life?

What must I let go of in order to dive deeper?

Who am I?

Do I love who I am?

What must I do in order to live authentically?

Why am I here?

If I were to die by midnight tonight, would what I'm doing now matter?

How can I be more honest and sincere?

What am I scared of?

What is keeping me from the Truth?

Does living a meaningful life have any meaning to me? What is this meaning?

How honest can I be with myself?

If the last email I sent were my very last, would I be okay with the message within?

If the last person I spoke with were my very last conversation, would I be okay with this interaction?

Do I feel peace in my life? If not, why?

What keeps me up at night?

What is tugging at my heart? Lying heavy upon my soul?

Do I engage with other Truth-seekers? Are they my closest friends? Am I my own best friend?

Do I have a tendency to defend? To argue? To provide reasons, explanations or justifications? Why?

What is my attitude towards seeking the Truth?

How open will I allow myself to be?

Where do I need to go and what do I need to do in order to be healthier, in mind, body and spirit? To have balance, peace and compassion in my heart?

Can I show more of myself to the world? What am I hiding? Why?

What is my intention in what I'm about to do today?

What is my purpose in the work I do or the art I create?

Do I feel a need to always be productive? Efficient? Busy? Why?

How am I validating myself? Is it through others? Is it through labels or roles? Why?

How am I receiving encouragement and support? From what sources? Are these sources healthy and best for me?

How am I treating myself today? Am I taking good care of my spirit?

How do I view myself?

When I look in the mirror, do I recognize the person looking back at me?
If not, why is this?

Why is Truth important to me?

SELECTED RECOMMENDED READINGS

When Things Fall Apart by Pema Chödrön
Man's Search for Meaning by Viktor E. Frankl
Into the Wild by Jon Krakauer
Truth and Untruth by Friedrich Nietzsche
Zen and the Art of Motorcycle Maintenance by Robert M. Pirsig
Walden by Henry David Thoreau

ACKNOWLEDGEMENTS

There have been many folks past and present who have tremendously inspired me in my life philosophy, how I approach creativity and art, spirituality and existential meaning. Here I name but a few: Paul Arden, Pema Chödrön, Epictetus, Flynn, Jack Kerouac, Jon Krakauer, Christopher Johnson McCandless, Robert M. Pirsig, Ayn Rand, and Henry David Thoreau.

ABOUT THE AUTHOR

Nina Yau has been writing since the age of five. With a penchant for adventure, she completed her first international flight alone at age six to Taiwan (Republic of China) with nothing more than a small duffel bag and a stuffed kitten in tow. After completing business school in her hometown of Chicago and well into a standard corporate life, Nina chose to leave the 9-to-5 lifestyle in order to live a life more suited to her spirit.

Nina helps others discover the Truth within all of us through teaching Yoga and with her introspective writings at her blog www.castlesintheair.org.

Made in the USA
Lexington, KY
20 November 2012